CW01667918

# Spy Dogs

# The Dog Who Loved Me

Story by Sefton Greene

Illustrations by Geri Kelly

# DEDICATION

This book is dedicated to all the Spy Dogs out there.

CONTENTS

# CHAPTER ONE

*Heathrow Airport, London, England, a few years from now.*

Mike Wild was sat waiting for the next plane to Sydney, Australia. He had been asked to set off the fireworks to let the New Year in, and couldn't wait. It was their summer there, and would be a nice change from the cold, wet weather of London.

A voice came on over the tannoy to announce the flight to Sydney would now be boarding. Wild stood, grabbed his bag and headed towards the gate. However, just as he set off he thought he had heard someone call his name. He looked around, saw nobody there and decided to ignore it. He probably wasn't the only Mike Wild in that airport.

"Wild! Wild! WILD!" he heard someone almost scream

behind him. He whipped back around to see his friend, Miss Hat Dog come hurtling towards him, waving her passport and a ticket. She almost jumped over a holidaymaker to get to Wild, whilst everyone stared at her in her pink hat and dress. Her golden brown hair tumbled over her beautiful face, and she pushed it out of her eyes before waving to Mike. Wild had to admit though, she did look like a million bones.

"What are you doing her Hat Dog? What has happened?" Wild asked with a puzzled expression on his face.

"Nothing!" she replied, in an almost sing-song voice. "I just didn't want to miss the plane".

"Plane? Are you going on holiday too?"

"No silly. I'm coming with you to Sydney."

"You can't come with me Hat Dog! I'll get in trouble".

"Aw please let me come Wild. I'll rub your belly and make you a three egg omelette. I'll even make it my New Year's resolution, so I have to stick to it!"

Mike could never say no to Hat Dog and she knew it. He reluctantly nodded, knowing this would come back to haunt him in one way or another. She squealed and grabbed Mike in a hug that almost suffocated him. "Ok Hat Dog, lets get on this plane," Mike wheezed as he wrestled himself out of her grip. She let go and they proceeded to head towards the plane.

After boarding, Wild and Hat Dog sat up front with their dog water and a three egg omelette for Wild. Mike kept catching a glimpse of two dogs sat about four rows behind him, who looked extremely familiar. He didn't want to approach them in case he was wrong. He didn't think that there could be anything more embarrassing! He noticed that they had been constantly looking at Hat Dog, but he didn't think this was particularly strange as most dogs did this all the time. He decided to ignore the two dogs, and quickly forgot about them. Instead he settled down to watch a film with Hat Dog, before swiftly falling asleep to the sounds of her soft singing of *'Hopelessly Devoted to You'*.

# CHAPTER TW0

*Sydney Harbour Bridge, Australia, New Years Eve.*

So far, Sydney had been amazing. Wild and Hat Dog had visited the Opera House, Bondi Beach, and were finally waiting to set off the fireworks over Sydney Harbour Bridge. They were extremely excited to set off the fireworks at midnight, and couldn't wait to let the New Year in. The mayor of Sydney strode up to Wild and introduced himself while swarms of helicopters flew around the bridge, and lights flashed. Crowds of dogs had gathered, their faces bright with excitement

"…Yes mayor, both myself and Hat Dog are honoured to be here, aren't we Hat Dog?" Mike asked.

"…Hat Dog?" he asked again, a little louder this time. He looked around frantically. Where could she be?

Suddenly, Mike caught a glimpse of a familiar figure in the crowd. Calor Gas. He was unmistakable with his white fur, and black patch around his left eye and ear. He was also in his oversized blue suit and red bow tie. He always wore that outfit. Behind Calor Gas, Wild could see Shifty Eyes and Bandy, Calor Gas' henchdogs, holding Hat Dog. She was being kidnapped!

Calor Gas had hated Wild ever since he had first foiled his plans to become King of England (but that's another story for another time).

Calor Gas and his henchmen began to run to their helicopter in the distance, dragging Hat Dog along in the process. Mike had to think fast. The helicopter would take off any minute!

Quickly, Mike rushed towards the button he and Hat Dog would have pressed to let the fireworks off. Mike slammed his paw onto the button. Whiz! Bang! Whoosh! Brilliant flashes of light and colour went shooting high into the sky, exploding into the starry night. One of the fireworks hit the helicopter that had now taken off, holding Calor Gas and Hat Dog. The helicopter started to spin out of control, and had to make an emergency landing at the bottom of Sydney Harbour Bridge.

Mike started to climb down to the helicopter. He hoped that Hat Dog was okay. The door to the helicopter burst open and Calor Gas and his henchdogs wrestled Hat Dog out of the wreckage and threw her into a nearby car, before setting off at high speed. Mike couldn't climb down fast enough to reach them. By the time he had reached the bottom, they had gone. Mike Wild stood in the cloud of dust left behind by the fleeing car and shouted after Calor Gas, 'I don't know who you think you are Calor Gas, or what you want, but I think you have forgotten. I have a set of skills that you could never dream of. Skills I have worked on over the years. Skills that mean I will never stop. Know this Calor Gas," Wild was practically screaming by this point as the car was nearly out of sight, "I will find you Calor Gas, and I will kill you. If it's the last thing I ever do!"

# CHAPTER THREE

*London, United Kingdom, twenty four hours later. At the Control Centre, Code Name: Head Kennel.*

Mike Wild strolled into the British Chief of Dog's office. D's secretary, Miss Wagtail was there. "Hi Mike. D is expecting you. I'll just ring through to let him know you are here". Mike laid down on the leather sofa opposite Miss Wagtail's desk. He closed his eyes and waited for that familiar shout from D's office.

"MIKE WILD! GET IN HERE NOW!" There it was. Wild hopped off of the sofa, gave Miss Wagtail a wink on the way past and swaggered into D's office.

D was sat behind his desk. His long face, always had a sour, grumpy look to it when Wild was around. As soon as

Wild stepped into D's office, his boss began to shout so loud and for so long it seemed as if there was steam coming out of his long floppy ears. Wild stood there with a grin on his face.

"Where on earth is Hat Dog?! She should not have been in Sydney with you, she was supposed to be working on a top secret mission in Germany! Well, what do you have to say? Wild? What went wrong?"

"Calor Gas. That's what went wrong". Wild replied.

"You have to get her back. Calor Gas has made a ransom demand for one million bones."

"One million!" gasped Wild.

"Yes, one million. Has your hearing gone Wild? So… the plan is simple. Rescue Hat Dog before we have to pay Calor Gas. There is an envelope on the desk. The code name is 'The Dog Who Loved Me'."

D continued, "we believe Calor Gas is in Monte Carlo, so you must prepare to go there tonight. But first, go meet with Twig; he has some gadgets for your mission…oh, and Wild…behave yourself."

Wild walked across the yard to Twig branch to get the gadgets for his mission. He opened the door and sauntered inside. Twig was stood in his office at Twig Branch in his long white laboratory coat. "Hi, Twig," Mike called.

"Don't 'hi Twig' me. Where are my gadgets from the China mission?"

"Yes…well…you know…" Wild started.

"Oh, be quiet Wild, and pay attention. I will say this only once. The first gadget is a new pair of trainers, but these are no ordinary trainers, these are oil slick trainers. If you click your heels, oil spills out of the back, making it virtually impossible for anyone to catch up with you."

"Oh, good," said Wild, "I'll be able to slip away."

"Be quiet Wild and put these trainers on." Wild did as he was told. "Okay," Twig continued, "next up I have a new pen for you. This pen however, sends smoke out of the nib. It provides you with a smokescreen that will make you almost invisible."

"Let me have a look," Wild said.

"No!" replied Twig, "not today. Keep your paws off it

because I have a new car for you to go to Monte Carlo in. Its a convertible sports car. I even have it in your favourite colour, Wild, red. This is one of the fastest cars on the road. Oh…and Wild…don't press the switch unless you have too. It's a turbo switch, so it will make you go really fast."

Wild jumped into the car with his pen and trainers, saying, "thanks Twig. I will return these gadgets to you in one piece." He started the car. "Goodbye Twig, I'll be back." As he said this, he pushed the turbo switch and smashed through the wall of Twig Branch. Twig put his paws to his face and groaned, "oh, please behave yourself Wild."

# CHAPTER FOUR

*Isle of Dogs, London, United Kingdom.*

Wild was driving through the City of London in the new car when he decided he would need to make a few stops before he went to Monte Carlo. He was getting hungry so his first stop would be his favourite restaurant, the world famous Brown Dog, in north London.

Within a few minutes, Wild was outside the Brown Dog; he pulled up and jumped out of the car. As he entered the restaurant, he was greeted by two new waiters, who he had never seen before. The tallest of the two spoke, "Hi, Wild, Mike Wild…your usual today, sir?"

"Yes please, a glass of dog water with ice and omelette please," Wild replied.

"Of course, Mr. Wild. Please take a seat and it will be with you in a moment." Wild took a seat and stared at the new waiters. He felt as if he had seen them both somewhere before. One of the waiters brought his drink. It tasted perfect. Next his omelette arrived, however, there was something wrong. Wild usually had three eggs in his omelette but this one tasted as if there were two.

Suddenly, Mike realised. These new waiters, were Shifty Eyes and Bandy. Calor Gas' henchdogs! Just as Mike stood up to leave, Bandy raced over to the table and tried to grab Wild, who ducked and pressed the button on his smoke pen. Something was wrong. The pen had released far more smoke than it should of done, to the point were no-one could seen anyone at all. Wild dropped to the floor and crawled out on his paws and knees. Shifty Eyes and Bandy were coughing and swinging their arms wildly around. They shouted, "Wild, were are you?"

Wild emerged outside and jumped into his red sports car. He pressed the turbo switch and set off at high speed. He reflected on the events that had just unfolded. It was a good job that the smoke pen had been faulty; it had actually saved him from being caught.

Once Wild was certain he had escaped, he turned the turbo switch off and drove at a normal speed. "Well," he said to himself out loud. "That was a close one. I had better go home and collect my tooth brush before I head off to Monte Carlo."

Mike lived at number 1, Wood Wharf in London. After pulling into his garage, Wild noticed that the door to his house was open. Wild carefully walked into his house, closing the door behind him. He headed straight for the bathroom to pick up his toothbrush. Suddenly, a noise from the kitchen made him whip round and run downstairs. "Who's there?" Mike asked.

"It's me, Miss Wagtail. You forgot your tickets for the Hovercraft to France."

"Good thinking Miss Wagtail."

"Please take me with you Mike. Let me come with you to France. I've never been on a mission before, and I really want to go."

"I am afraid that is not possible Miss Wagtail. D has to say it is okay, and he needs your help here in London. However, I expect we could have glass of dog water or two before I go."

As Wild started to make the perfect glass of dog water for Miss Wagtail, he heard a noise outside; someone was throwing stones at his window. He went to investigate and was just about to throw a drink over whoever was throwing stones, when he saw it was D.

"Wild!" shouted D. "Open your door and let me in. We need to talk, and by the way, you haven't seen Miss Wagtail, have you?"

Wild froze, then replied, "No…have you?"

"Me?" said D, "well I wouldn't be asking you, would I? Stop fooling around and open the door".

"Ok," agreed Wild, "just on my way, D."

Mike slammed the window shut and rushed over to Miss Wagtail. "Hide, quick. D is outside and he is wondering where you are. Quick, hide behind the door and be quiet." Wild suggested.

Mike raced downstairs and opened the door for D. "So, D. What brings you here?"

"Calor Gas has demanded another million bones. And this time, he wants the Queen's bones!"

"What?! Another million bones? and the Queen's ones too?" gasped Wild. "So that makes two million bones in total?"

"Yes Wild," murmured D. "I didn't know you could count. He wants it by tomorrow night, so you better hurry. He will be waiting at the Casino in Casino Square in Monte Carlo. He wants you to take the bones in person. You must come with me now to collect the bones from the bank. Oh, and also, before I forget, Twig has given me a new mobile phone for you to take to Monte Carlo. Apparently it works on the moon."

"I'm sure that will come in useful when I'm in Monte Carlo, won't it?" sniggered Mike.

"Oh do be quiet Wild," D complained. He was just about to leave when he caught sight of the two glasses of dog water that Mike had made for himself and Miss Wagtail. "Wild? Why are there two glasses of dog water? Were you entertaining or something? Was Wagtail here?"

"No," replied Wild. "I haven't seen her since I was in your

office this morning."

"Hmm.. I wonder where she could be then?" D asked. "Anyway, Wild we must get on; you have a hovercraft to catch in Dover in a little over an hour, so we better get moving."

They left Wild's house and headed towards the Bank of Bones in the city. Stopping his car Wild jumped out and opened the boot and the manager of the Bank of Bones brought the two million bones out of the bank in a sealed treasure box. He handed the key to Mike whilst D put the box in the boot of his car. "We cannot afford to lose these bones Wild', D explained. "Don't worry. I will bring Hat Dog back and still have the bones." "Just no slip ups Wild. Please," begged D as he handed the mobile phone that works on the moon to Wild. "I'll be heading to France too, to oversee the operation. Remember to keep your phone on so we can contact you. Oh and Wild…don't fool around".

Mike jumped into his sports car and sped off, pressing the turbo switch as he set off. D put his head in his hands and groaned. Wild had better behave himself.

# CHAPTER FIVE

*On the road to Dover, United Kingdom.*

Wild was on his way to Dover to catch the Hovercraft with the two million bones in the boot of his car. 'This was the life', Mike thought. He had the open road ahead of him, a nice summer's day and his favourite band, The Huskies, playing from the car radio. Within an hour or so, the White Cliffs of Dover sprang into view, and the hovercraft he was to board.

Once on the hovercraft, Wild made his way onto the deck and to the restaurant on the second floor. As he entered the waitress walked over to him and recognised him instantly. "Wild?! Mike Wild?" she practically shouted.

"Yes," Mike mumbled back, slightly embarrassed. These

days he couldn't go anywhere without someone recognising him. "Three egg omelette and a glass of dog water for you Mr Wild?" the waitress asked enthusiastically. Mike nodded and made his way to a table in the far corner. He didn't have to wait long before his meal arrived. It was perfect.

By this point the hovercraft was well on it's way to France, and Mike could hear music in the distance. It sounded like a disco! Wild left the restaurant and made his way to the first floor. Wild could see that there was indeed a disco, and the dance floor was packed. Mike weaved his way between the dancing dogs and started to dance. They were playing a Huskies song.

Wild was dancing away when two very familiar dogs walked through the crowd, straight towards him. 'Oh no', though Wild. It was Shift Eyes and Bandy Legs, Calor Gas' henchdogs. Shifty and Bandy went to grab him, but Wild ducked and dropped to the floor, face down. Wild then felt a tugging at his legs. They had him! Wild knew exactly what to do. He clicked his heels and oil from his oil slick trainers sprayed out, all over Shifty and Bandy. Their faces were black as the oil temporarily blinded them so Mike could get away.

There was oil everywhere, Mike realised as he fled the dance floor. Shifty and Bandy were behind him, sliding around, attempting to gain their balance. Suddenly, Mike reached the end of the dance floor and realised it was a dead end. Oh no! The only way out was back past Calor Gas' henchdogs. Wild had to come up with a plan soon.

Wild started to run straight at Shifty Eyes and Bandy Legs, who were still preoccupied with attempting to stand upright. Mike barged past the two of them, pushing them both to the ground before racing through the door that led to the upper deck. He could feel Calor Gas' henchdogs, right behind him. They backed Mike into a corner, both began to grin. "We've got you now", Shifty Eyes, exclaimed excitedly.

"We've managed to trap the famous Mike Wild, Mr. Gas will be really pleased about this!" laughed Bandy Legs.

Mike looked about frantically, there had to be a way out. There always was. Suddenly, Mike caught a glimpse of a pole hanging about Shifty Eyes' head. Mike knew what he needed to do. "Unfortunately, my ugly friends, today is not the day that you managed to catch Mike Wild." As he said this, Mike jumped onto the pole, swung around and kicked both Shifty Eyes and Bandy Legs over the side of the hovercraft. They landed in the water.

Mike expertly landed back on his feet and looked over the side. He threw two rubber rings down to them and shouted, "see you in France! Have a nice swim."

# CHAPTER SIX

*From Calais to Paris, France.*

As Wild drove from the Hovercraft onto the Calais dock, he noticed three of the dogs from the French Spy Dogs organisation. "Bonjour, Mr Wild, welcome to France," said the French Chief of Dogs. Wild's French had always been shockingly bad, and so replied to the French Chief of Dogs by asking for some bread and a hairdryer. "Quite so," the French Chief of Dogs replied, with a puzzled expression. "Erm, anything else we can help you with?" the chief of Dogs continued. Wild, meaning to ask for some more oil cartridges to place in his shoes, instead asked for a plastic duck and some ear muffs. "But of course Wild," replied the French Chief of Dogs, "we are here to help". "Gracias," Wild replied and jumped into his sports car. He pressed the turbo switch, leaving the port of Calais far behind him. The French Chief of Dogs was left standing there, ordering his employees to gather some French bread, a hairdryer, a plastic duck and some ear muffs, and send them to Mike for when he arrived in Paris.

Wild was flicking through the French radio stations when he saw a sign saying Paris, 150km. He couldn't wait to get there and rest. D had organised the penthouse at the George V hotel in the city centre. There would even be a bottle of dog water there, the '82 vintage. His favourite.

Whilst Wild was daydreaming about the wonderful hotel he would be arriving at soon, he noticed a familiar black car behind him. Shifty Eyes and Bandy Legs! They must have been following him all the way from Calais. Before he knew it, the car had smashed into the back of him, forcing Wild to jolt forward in his seat. Wild pushed the turbo switch again, but something seemed wrong with it. Nothing was happening. Wild hadn't realised that the turbo switch had stopped working between here and Calais, he had been too busy thinking about Paris. Wild put his paw down and accelerated. Calor Gas' henchdogs were still catching up with him. They pulled alongside Wild. Bandy

Legs was driving, and Shifty Eyes had started to climb out of his seat. He was going to try to jump onto Wild's car!

Looking ahead, Wild noticed that they were coming up to a single lane tunnel. He glanced across to see Bandy Legs looking back at him. They were obviously thinking the same thing. Who would get through the tunnel first? Wild or the henchdogs? Wild suddenly picked up a bottle of dog water he had on the seat next to him. Quick as a flash he flicked the lid off and threw water over Bandy, who let go of the steering wheel in an attempt to dry his eyes. This forced Shifty Eyes, to tumble out of the car into the road and Bandy Legs swerved to avoid hitting his fellow henchdog. Wild accelerated through the tunnel before seeing Bandy Legs in the rearview mirror, crash into a pile of dog poo in a field at the side of the road. He was covered from head to paw. "We will get you Wild", Mike heard them shout.

'Not before you've had a bath, you wont', Mike chuckled to himself.

Further down the road, Mike thought about how close that encounter was. He would have to get that turbo switch fixed. Settling back into his seat, he turned the radio up and sped on.

Just outside of Paris, Mike realised he needed fuel and pulled over into the nearest service station. Just as he had finished filling up, his phone that works on the moon rang. It was D. "What have you been up to Wild? There's apparently oil all over the hovercraft and the French Chief of Dogs tells me you asked him to get plastic ducks and hairdryers! What's happening? Where are you right now?"

"Oh, sorry sir, I can't hear you. Must be a bad line..hello," Wild hung up on D. Plastic Ducks! Wild thought. D must have me confused with another case.

Wild walked into the service station to pay, picked up a bottle of dog water and a pair of sunglasses at the same time, returned to his car and decided he would just rest his eyes for a while.

# CHAPTER SEVEN

*Meanwhile in Monte Carlo, France.*

Calor Gas had always loved the view from his mountain top hideout in Monte Carlo. He could see the sea from here. It glistened. Sometimes he would even pretend that he could hear its gentle waves, as a way of calming himself down whenever he thought about Mike Wild.

The dog had plagued him ever since he had foiled his plans to become King of England. Calor Gas had been so close. The archbishop had almost placed that glorious crown upon his head, before Wild snatched it out of his grasp, forcing Calor Gas into hiding. Calor Gas had to kidnap Hat Dog to teach Wild a lesson. Calor Gas was not a dog to be messed with.

He hadn't been harsh to Hat Dog. He wasn't a monster after all. He hadn't kept her locked up in the basement with ropes around her paws and tape over her snout. In truth, he had given her a free run of all the facilities, including the swimming pool, jacuzzi and sauna. Hat Dog was in no rush to be rescued. But Wild would come, there was no doubt about that. When Wild finally did show up, Calor Gas would be waiting to destroy him.

His evil plan could not fail.

# CHAPTER EIGHT

*Back at the Service Station just outside Paris, France.*

As Wild slept, Shifty and Bandy had pulled into the services so Bandy could clean himself up after crashing into the dog poo. Bandy ran to the toilets to find that they were locked. All the other dogs around him were holding their noses, and Bandy began to feel embarrassed.

Meanwhile, Shifty had been sitting in the car, waiting for Bandy to hurry up. All of a sudden, the tracker that the two henchdogs had secretly planted on Wild's car, back on the hovercraft, began to beep. Wild must be close. Bandy looked across the service station to see Wild's red sports car. "Oh yes! There he is Shifty. We've got him now. Come on let's go get him." Bandy exclaimed.

Shifty and Bandy dropped to their paws and knees and started to crawl across the car park to Wild's car. Wild was still asleep inside. Shifty and Bandy were almost at Wild's car, when Bandy's phone began to buzz. It was Calor Gas. "Hi boss,"

"Hi boss?" said Calor Gas, with noticeable anger in his voice. "Have you got Mike Wild yet?"

"Erm, nearly boss,"

"Listen to me. I will say this only once. Wild has two million bones in the boot of his car and you must get them for me. Don't come back without them. We need them for the plan. Wild will come to try to rescue Hat Dog anyway without the bones and I simply won't release her. At this rate anyway, Wild is going to have to drag Hat Dog away from me. She's falling in love with me, I can see it in her face. Oh how I cannot wait for Wild to find out his precious Hat Dog doesn't like him anymore. Anyway," Calor Gas continued, "get me those bones!"

"Ok boss," Shifty said and hung up.

Whilst Calor Gas had been relaying his instructions to his henchdogs, Wild had started to awaken. He could smell an awful smell, almost like dog poo. Suddenly, a noise from behind him made him sit up. It was Shifty and Bandy! Of course, that's where that smell has come from, Wild thought to himself. The two henchdogs were proceeding to try to break into the boot of his car. They were trying to steal the bones! "Oh no you don't," Wild though aloud. He started the car and slammed his paw onto the turbo switch.

Unfortunately for Shifty and Bandy, Wild had been parked on gravel. His tyres span as he headed off at high speed, leaving Bandy covered in dog poo and stones. Wild could see Shifty laughing at Bandy in his rearview mirror, and Bandy stormed off, before losing sight of them completely.

After a few hours of driving, Wild could finally see the Eiffel Tower in the distance. "Paris at last", he exclaimed. Wild was already planning what he would do whilst in the city. He would have to visit his favourite tailor and get a new suit. Whilst Wild was thinking about what colour of suit to get, when the phone that works on the moon began to ring.

"Hello," Wild said

"Hello, it's the French Chief of Dogs here. I will meet you in the bar at your hotel at 8:30pm tonight. Be sharp Wild!"

Wild decided to reply to the Chief of Dogs in French, but accidentally said 'plastic duck' instead of 'I'll be there'. Wild hung up before the French Chief of Dogs could reply.

# CHAPTER NINE

*Paris, France.*

When Wild reached Paris, he was reminded suddenly of Hat Dog. He had met her in Paris whilst she had been working there as a model. He'd seen her at fashion week and fallen instantly in love with her. They had had dates on top of the Eiffel tower, sat outside Notre Dame and gone shopping on the Champs-Élysées. This city lived and breathed memories of Hat Dog.

It wasn't a lie to say that Wild was almost relived when he arrived at his hotel. Here he could attempt to hide from these memories for a while. He took the cases of bones with him into the reception area and checked in. "We've been expecting you Mr. Wild." The Hotel manager spoke, "It's been a long time. Where have you been?"

"Oh, here and there," replied Wild. He asked the manager to give him a wake up call at 8pm so he could go and meet the French Chief of Dogs in the bar. "Certainly," said the manager. "Your penthouse is ready for you and we will keep a close eye on your car."

Wild thanked him, picked up his cases and headed towards the lift. He checked his watch to see that it was 6pm. He had plenty of time for a quick forty winks or so.

As Mike was looking at his watch, the lift door opened to reveal a bell puppy. He was extremely short and had bouncy golden curls that circled his head. His little blue bell boy hat was perched on top of them, at an angle, and matched his blue uniform. "Going up to the penthouse, Mr. Wild?" he asked.

"Of course," Wild replied, "to the top!"

The doors of the lift closed and they started to move up at high speed. The lift reached the top floor in no time and the doors opened. Wild thanked the bell puppy

"No problem Mr. Wild. If you need anything, and I mean anything, just press the button on this remote control," the puppy said as he threw the remote into Wild's outstretched paws. Wild looked at the puppy who winked at him before stepping back into the lift and leaving Wild to ponder over the remote. "Why did he give me this?" Wild asked himself. "Well, I suppose I'll find out at some point," Wild shrugged and placed the remote in his pocket.

Inside the room, Wild admired the views over Paris, before noting that the penthouse had the biggest bed Wild had ever seen. Climbing onto the bed, he allowed himself to have a small jump up and down before grabbing a bottle of '82 dog water that had been placed on the sideboard. Wild was about to shake the bottle and spray it everywhere before a voice from behind made him jump. "Wild! What are you doing?" Twig barked.

"What are you doing here Twig?" Mike replied.

"I've come to help you."

"Help me?"

"Yes. We have had information that you're being tracked. Calor Gas' henchdogs must have placed a tracking device on your car when you got onto the hovercraft at Dover."

"That explains a lot," Wild said.

"Anyway, some of the boys in the lab have changed the ringtone on your phone that works on the moon."

"What have they changed it too?" Wild asked, not really understanding why it had been necessary to change the ringtone.

"I don't know Wild, I just thought I would warn you. I'd also like to know how my gadgets are doing?"

"Fine," lied Wild. "I haven't used any yet."

"Ah, good!" Twig smiled. "I better be off Wild. Remember to behave yourself with my gadgets. I need them back," Twig warned before leaving Wild alone in the penthouse.

# CHAPTER TEN

*Meanwhile in Monte Carlo, France.*

Calor Gas was getting fed up with his useless henchdogs, Shifty and Bandy. They had failed on numerous occasions to capture Wild or the bones. Every opportunity they wasted, brought Wild closer to Calor Gas and Hat Dog.

Luckily for Calor Gas, Hat Dog didn't know that Wild was attempting to rescue her. She was too busy driving around Monte Carlo and spending hours on Calor Gas's yacht.

Calor Gas knew he had to do something exceptional now to stop Wild and to keep Hat Dog and the bones for ever.

# CHAPTER ELEVEN

*Back in Paris, France.*

There was a knock at Mike Wild's hotel door. Wild awoke from his nap and sprang out of bed. "It's your wake up call," Mike heard the bell puppy shout through the door. Wild was groggy from his sleep and decided to jump into the shower to wake himself up before his meeting with the French Chief of Dogs.

Whilst Wild was taking his shower however, Shifty and Bandy had been downstairs in the hotel's boiler room, adding bulbs of garlic to the water tank. They hoped that Wild would now stink as much as Bandy had earlier. Wild had no idea about what was happening and happily continued singing and dancing in the shower. It wasn't until Wild dried himself that he thought he could detect a strange smell coming from somewhere. Wild shrugged his shoulders and continued getting ready.

When Wild had finished getting ready, he called the lift and stepped inside. Of course, the bell puppy was there, ready to press the button for Wild. "Going down Mr. Wild?" the puppy asked.

"Yes, thank you," Wild replied. The two stood in silence for a few seconds, and Mike could see, out of the corner of his eye, the bell puppy sniffing the air. "Mr. Wild," the bell puppy began, "can you smell something? Quite strong, almost like garlic?" Wild sniffed the air, but he couldn't smell anything. He decided to ignore the bell puppy's question and continued staring at the lift door. As they reached the bottom, the doors opened and Mike stepped out of the lift. "Mr. Wild, I hope you still have that remote I gave you," the bell puppy called after him. Wild took the remote out of his pocket, held it up to the puppy and walked off to the bar.

On his way into the hotel bar, Wild noticed that there were quite a few dogs holding their snouts, but he continued to ignore them and went and sat next to the French Chief of Dogs. "Ah, Wild," the French Chief of Dogs said. Wild replied by saying 'plastic duck' in French, to which the French Chief of Dogs shook his head and continued, "can I get you a drink?"

"Yes of course," said Wild. "I'll have dog water in a tall glass, please."

"Make that two, bardog," said the Chief. "By the way, I've booked a table at the Champs de Mars in the Eiffel Tower."

"Good," said Wild, a little less enthusiastically than he probably should have done. That was the restaurant he and Hat Dog had been to on their first date. "I believe it's the best restaurant in Paris," Wild continued.

The Chief told Wild to drink up so they could head to dinner. "How are we going to get to the restaurant?" Wild asked. "Taxi?"

"No, there is only one way to travel in Paris," replied the Chief. "Come on, I'll show you."

Wild started to walk from the hotel to where the Chief had transport waiting. When he saw it he turned to the Chief and said, "Is this a joke?" Wild found himself staring at two motorbikes. He climbed onto the nearest one and clipped his helmet in place. "You know, a taxi would have been fine," Mike mumbled to the Chief, who fortunately couldn't hear him because he'd switched his engine on and was already pulling out onto the street.

A few minutes into the journey, Wild noticed the familiar black car of Shifty and Bandy. "I think we have company," Mike shouted to the French Chief of Dogs, who couldn't hear him because of the loud roar of the motorbike engine and the general noise of the city. Mike sighed and continued following the Chief to the Eiffel Tower.

The Eiffel Tower loomed over them when they approached. Wild could see small planes flying around the top of it. It was so big, it broke through the little, fluffy clouds.

They pulled up at the bottom of the tower, where there were dogs selling souvenirs and gifts. Wild looked around and saw a dog selling sun glasses with the Eiffel Tower on the side of them. He wanted some so he walked up to the dog, bought them and put them on. He looked very silly as he walked back to the French Chief of Dogs. "This is not a game Wild," the Chief scolded. "Please remember why we are here. You look stupid."

"But I'm undercover, I need to blend in with the other holidaymakers here," Wild replied.

"Yes, great disguise," sniffed the Chief. "Come on, let's take the lift to the restaurant."

They walked over to the lift, leaving their motorbikes at the bottom of the tower. There were a lot of dogs waiting to go to the top and when the doors opened, they all got in. The lift was soon full and the doors began to close. The lift moved slowly upwards. Wild noticed that the other dogs in the lift had started to screw their faces up. "What's that smell?" Wild heard one small puppy say to his mum.

"It's like garlic," she replied to her son.

When the lift reached the top, Wild and the French Chief of Dogs got out. "Could you smell anything?" Wild asked the Chief.

"Yes," replied the Chief, "it was a strong smell, whatever it was."

The pair walked into the restaurant, where they were greeted by the manager. "Good Evening Chief. I see you have brought Mr. Wild with you today," the manger exclaimed. "It's a pleasure to have you here Mr. Wild."

The manager showed them to the best table in the restaurant, that had views over all of Paris. "Mr Wild," the manager began, "I was just wondering what aftershave you are wearing. It smells so nice, so fresh."

"Erm," Wild stammered. He wasn't wearing any aftershave.

"I'm glad someone likes it," murmured the Chief as they sat down.

"I'll have the omelette and your best bottle of dog water," Mike told the manager, who quickly scurried off to get it.

Meanwhile, Wild and the French Chief of Dogs were enjoying the views of Paris. "Look at those two fellows down there," the Chief pointed. It was Shifty and Bandy. Bandy was still covered in dog poo and gravel. "Look at the state of them," the Chief continued.

"You do know that they are Calor Gas' henchdogs?" Wild asked. "They are probably following me, thinking that I have the bones."

"What?" gasped the Chief, "look Wild, I have to go," the

French Chief of Dogs said as he quickly left the restaurant. By the time Wild looked around, the Chief was out of the door.

'Well, wasn't he useful?' Mike thought to himself. Wild sat wondering what to do, before looking out of the window again to see that even more henchdogs had joined Shifty and Bandy. There must have been around twenty or more. Wild was surrounded.

The manager walked up to his table with his omelette and dog water. "Here you are, sir," he said, "what about the Chief? Will he be wanting his dinner? I saw him leave quite quickly." Wild explained that the Chief had gone before the manager informed him that there were dogs outside asking about him.

Wild thanked the manager, took his sunglasses off and tucked into his omelette. It was the best he had ever tasted. He put his head down and wondered what he was going to do.

Suddenly, his phone that works on the moon rang. Back at headquarters they had changed the ring tone to, 'Hopelessly Devoted to You,' Hat Dog's favourite song.

Wild smiled and answered the phone.

"Hello," Mike said. There was no one on the other line. Wild thought this was strange. He hung up and put it back in his pocket. Just as he did this however, he noticed the remote that the bell puppy had given him. The bell puppy's instructions were to press the button if he needed help. Well, this was certainly a situation in which he could use a little help. Mike pressed the button and waited for something to happen.

All of a sudden, a helicopter appeared at the window. The henchdogs had, by this point, made it into the restaurant, ready to capture Wild. Whilst they were distracted by the helicopter, Wild saw an opportunity to run past them and up the tower. Step after step, up and up he went, whilst the twenty henchdogs quickly followed him. Wild was running fast to reach the top but he had no plan for when he got there. As he ran he clicked his heels and oil spurted out of the back of his trainers all over the steps.

The first dog hit the oil and fell backwards onto the next dog, making them all fall one by one. Wild just laughed and shouted, "Yes!"

He soon reached the top and looked at the helicopter, wondering who was flying it. All he could see was a pair of sunglasses. He had to decide. Jump into the helicopter with someone he didn't know, or face the henchdogs who were currently picking themselves up and pulling themselves up the stairs towards Wild.

Wild made his decision. He jumped onto the helicopter. His legs dangling. The henchdogs tried to grab him as the helicopter moved up and away from the Eiffel Tower. "Thanks a lot," Wild said, a little out of breath.

"That's ok Mr. Wild," replied a little voice from the front seat of the helicopter. It was the bell puppy from the hotel! "You can fly a helicopter?" Wild asked, impressed.

"Of course, Mr. Wild. I'm Spy Puppy. They are training me to be just like you Mr. Wild," the excited puppy squealed.

A few minutes later, Spy Puppy landed the helicopter and they both got out. Wild thanked the little puppy for rescuing him. Just as he was thanking the puppy however, Shifty and Bandy came running towards them. "Quick!" Mike shouted, as he dashed towards his motorbike. "Jump on," Mike told the puppy.

"One minute Mr. Wild," the puppy shouted as he ran off. Where was he going?

Spy puppy ran into the park where there were puppies skating. There was one puppy on a board which only had two wheels. Spy Puppy ran up to him and asked for his board. "No way," the puppy said, "you can't have my board." Just at this moment however, Wild pulled up on his bike. "Are you with Mike Wild?" the puppy asked, amazed.

"Yes I am," Spy Puppy replied. As he said this, the puppy thrust his board into spy puppy's hands and ran off, before Spy puppy jumped onto the back of Wilds bike.

Just as they began to zoom off, Mike caught a glimpse of Shifty and Bandy climbing into the helicopter. "Oh no!" he cried as Shifty and Bandy began to ascend in the helicopter. They were right behind them. The two spies swayed from side to side but Shifty and Bandy were right above them, just missing them each time.

Wild looked to the right and saw a tunnel coming up. He told the puppy they were heading for it. They swerved quickly and the helicopter just missed them before they raced into the tunnel. Shifty and Bandy had to pull up to avoid crashing into the entrance of the tunnel.

It was completely dark in the tunnel. Wild flicked his light on and rode down. Shifty and Bandy hovered above where they could see both ends of the tunnel. They waited, knowing the spies had to come out. Wild and the puppy went about half way through, then stopped and got off the bike and board. "Well, that was a close one!" exclaimed the puppy. "But how are we going to get out?" he asked Wild.

Wild looked around and saw a hatch and said, "that's our way out. Leave the bike and bring the board."

They reached the hatch and slowly opened it. "Grr-what's that smell?" asked the puppy.

"It's dog poo," replied Wild. The hatch opened into a sewage pipe. "Quickly, use the board and we will float down the pipe."

"Do we have to?" asked the puppy.

"Yes, we must," said Wild, "or we will be caught by Shifty and Bandy."

He told the puppy to put a paw to his nose and jump on the board. They both landed on the board at the same time and floated down the pipe. The smell grew stronger as they went faster and faster. In the distance, Wild noticed some ladders, and in turn, their way out. He yelled to Spy Puppy, "grab my legs when I jump and grab the bottom of the ladder." The puppy grabbed Wild but they were both covered in dog poo, so the puppy had to hold on even harder. Wild climbed the ladder with the puppy hanging onto his legs. "We've lost the board," shouted the puppy.

"I'll buy you a new one, now come on. We have to get out of here," Wild told him.

Up and up Wild climbed, with the spy puppy holding on. They finally reached the top, where they had to push aside a big metal grate.

Mike poked his head up, looked around and saw they were in the middle of the Louvre art gallery. Mike clambered out and pulled the Spy Puppy up also. "How are we going to get out of here?" asked the puppy.

"Come on," replied Wild, "at least we are away from Shifty and Bandy."

As the two dogs proceeded to find the exit, Spy Puppy noticed the Mona Lisa Dog painting. "Don't touch it," Mike warned the puppy, but it was too late. As he spoke, Spy Puppy had already touched the painting and set the alarm system off. Wild put his paws to his ears. "I told you not to touch it!" he shouted.

In a matter of minutes, the two dogs were surrounded by French Police Dogs. "Well, well, what do we have here?" asked one.

"I can explain; it's not what you think," said Wild.

"Oh?" said the police dog, "I think you had better come with us."

"But I am Mike Wild. Just ask the French Chief of Dogs. He'll confirm who I am," pleaded Wild.

"You can explain yourself down at the station," said the police dog. "How on earth did you expect to get away with stealing that painting?"

"We weren't stealing it," Mike protested.

Wild and the puppy were lead out of the building into the back of the police van. They sat there looking at each other. “Don’t worry,” said Wild. “I have a friend called the Chief and he can fix anything.” The police dog overhead Wild and replied, “Oh, yes, and my name is the Queen of England.”

The van sped off, with sirens on, through the streets of Paris, to the police station. Just then the van began to swerve, and the engine began to whir. The driver had to pull over. “What’s happened?” asked the puppy.

“I don’t know,” replied Wild.

The police dog got out of the van and walked to the back, where he saw that he had a puncture.

“Does anyone know how to change a wheel?” he asked.

“Yes,” said the puppy, “I was a mechanic.”

“Oh good, you can help me,” said the police dog. He opened the van doors and Wild said, “I will help you too.” The police dog thanked him as Wild and the Spy Puppy headed to inspect the puncture. “You need a jack,” said Spy Puppy.

“What’s that?” asked the police dog. Spy puppy told him that it was for making the van go up so a tyre could be easily changed.

"It must be in the back of the van," said the police dog. He went round and climbed in and started to feel around. Wild looked at the puppy and they ran to the back of the van. They looked in and saw the police dog on his paws and knees. "It's just not your day, is it?" they asked. As they spoke, they slammed the door closed, locking him in the van.

The police dog put his paws to the bars in the back window. The two spies looked at him and said, "nothing personal, but we have a job to do."

They set off running before more police dogs arrived. They rounded a corner and saw a water fountain. "Quick, jump in," ordered Wild. "We might be able to get some of this dog poo off us." They both got in and ducked under the water and rubbed themselves down. When they climbed out of the water, they were greeted by two police dogs. "Hi," said Wild, "what's up?"

They told him they were looking for two dogs who had tried to steal a famous painting and had escaped from a police van. "And they are covered in dog poo," one of the police dogs said. “Have you seen them?”

“No,” said Wild, “We have just been having a swim. It is a very warm night after all.”

The police dogs told them that the dogs they are looking for had pretended to be Mike Wild and Spy Puppy. “But that’s us,” said Wild.

“I know,” said the Police dog, “you are the best spy dogs in the world.”

Wild thanked him then they both shook themselves dry, drenching the police dogs. “Sorry,” said Wild. “Come on, Puppy. If we see those dogs, we will let you know. By the way what do they look like?”

“They are about your height but covered in dog poo,” replied the police dog.

They then ran off as the sky was full of helicopters and TV cameras, all looking for two dogs who had tried to steal the Mona Lisa Dog. They were heading for the hotel when Wild’s phone that works on the moon, rang. ‘Hopelessly devoted to you’ blared out of the phone. “That’s your ringtone?” Spy Puppy asked.

"Don't ask," Wild replied. He clicked the answer button on the phone. "Hello, D, is that you?"

"Yes," came the reply. "What's going on? I'm watching TV and Paris is going mad."

"Someone's tried to steal the Mona Lisa Dog," explained Wild.

"You've got to be joking!" replied D. "I hope this has nothing to do with you."

"No, sir," replied Wild, "I'm just out having a walk around."

"Good," answered D. "Leave that to the French. It's none of our business. Do you still have the bones?"

"Yes, of course," said Wild.

"Well, good luck, and behave yourself down in Monte Carlo."

"Bye, sir."

Wild hung up and turned to Spy Puppy. "Come on, let's get back to the hotel."

As they walked into the hotel, the manager spoke to them about the crazy events that had been happening at the Louvre. "I can't believe someone tried to steal the Mona Lisa Dog!" the manager exclaimed.

"Yes, neither can I," said Wild. He made his excuses and headed with Spy Puppy up to the Penthouse. Once inside, Wild made himself some dog water and sat looking over the views of Paris, Spy Puppy at his side.

"So what is this job all about then Mr. Wild?" asked Spy Puppy. Wild told him about Hat Dog's kidnap by Calor Gas.

"Isn't she a model?" asked Spy Puppy.

"Yes, my dog friend, the dog who loves me."

"Listen Mr. Wild, I can help you. Where is she now?"

"Monte Carlo."

"I would like to go to Monte Carlo with you. You need my help," offered the puppy.

"You're a bit young yet though aren't you. To be helping on real missions?" asked Wild.

"I'm not too young!" protested Spy Puppy. "Look how useful I was tonight!"

"Well, if we are going together, you need to get some new clothes. We will visit my tailor in the morning," said Wild. "Oh, and by the way. What's your real name?"

"Smith. Eric Smith," replied the puppy.

"Well, it isn't the best spy dog name in the world, but it will do. Now go get some sleep. Tomorrow is going to be a long day." Eric started to head out of the penthouse. However, on his way, he turned around and asked Wild, "oh, by the way, can I drive to Monte Carlo tomorrow?"

"No," replied Wild.

"But I can fly helicopters and ride motorbikes and even skateboards," Eric protested.

"Go get some sleep Eric," Wild chuckled, "and thanks for your help today, at the Eiffel Tower."

"It's okay Mr. Wild. Goodnight," Eric said as he headed down in the Penthouse lift."

"Goodnight Eric," Mike smiled.

# CHAPTER TWELVE

*Paris, France, a few hours later.*

Eric woke Wild at 6:30am. "Come on Mr. Wild. We have a busy day today," Eric said in a bright, eager voice. Wild groaned, rolled over and picked up his phone to ring his tailor. "Hi," he said, "can you fit me in today?" The tailor said he could, but he should come round the back of the shop because the place was swarming with police dogs after someone had tried to steal the Mona Lisa Dog last night. "Ok, see you later," Wild said, and hung up.

A knock at the door, forced Wild to get up. "Room service," a voice sang through the door to the penthouse. The waiter brought in a lovely spread of food for Wild to eat, along with some puppy cereal and milk for Eric. Wild tucked into his omelette with three eggs, and it didn't take long for them to finish.

After getting properly ready and taking the bones out of their hiding place, Wild and Eric headed out to the tailor's. Wild strolled into the lift, putting his sunglasses on that he had bought from the Eiffel tower, the night before. Suddenly he stopped. "Let's take the stairs instead," insisted Mike.

"Why?" asked Eric

"I have a feeling. Call it a spy sense. You'll get it when you're older."

They headed to the stairs and walked down them, step by step, floor by floor. When they reached the bottom they were both out of breath, their tongues hanging out of their mouths. "Remind me why we did that Mr. Wild?" wheezed Eric.

"I don't know," said Wild, "but trust me, there was something not quite right about that lift today. Anyway, lets get my car. The manager has the keys." Mike said as they headed over to the reception. "Good morning Mr. Wild," the manager said brightly.

"Good morning," replied Wild and Eric.

"Are you checking out?"

"Yes, but we had a great time in Paris," Wild told him. "This hotel is the best in Paris."

"Thank you, sir. Where are you off to now?"

"We're on our way to Monte Carlo," said Wild. "May I have my keys?" The manager handed Wild his keys and wished him the best of luck.

Mike and Eric walked to the car. "Wow! What a car!" Eric exclaimed. "Please let me drive!"

"No, you're too young. I'm sorry. You must wait until you become a dog."

Wild started the car, lowered the roof and drove off listening to music. It was a lovely sunny day. Whilst they were driving along, Mike told Eric about the Tailor. The Tailor had a shop in every country in the world and could see into the future. He also of course made some of the best clothes around.

A few minutes later they pulled up at the back of the shop and walked to the door. Wild knocked and it opened very slowly, with a creaking noise. The dog that met them had a mane of shaggy grey hair that almost covered his eyes. This was in complete contrast to his blue suit, which was immaculate.

"Greetings," said the Tailor, rolling his tape measure around his paw.

"Hello," said Wild. "This is my friend Eric," he said, pushing the puppy forward to greet the Tailor. The pair shook hands and Wild followed them into the shop. "Wow!" exclaimed Eric. "There must be a suit for every occasion."

"Yes," said the Tailor. "Let me guess. You are going to Monte Carlo and you will be going to the casino, so you will want a tuxedo."

"How do you know?" asked Eric.

"It's my job," replied the Tailor. "And I know what sizes you are too." He paused, "I will get your tuxes and you will need some espadrilles for your paws. You will be the smartest dogs in Monte Carlo."

Wild thanked him and asked him if he could see into the future. The tailor nodded, then put his paws to his belt and began to waggle his hips. “Hmm, yes.” he said. “I can see you now. There is going to be a car chase. It’ll be a difficult car chase, but you will come out of it ok.”

Wild thanked the Tailor, who gave them his suits and shoes and said goodbye to the Tailor, until next time.

# CHAPTER THIRTEEN

*On the road to Monte Carlo.*

They soon picked up the signs for Monte Carlo, but they had a long way to go. Wild asked Eric if he would like some music on.

"Yes, please. Have you got 'Dogs Aloud'?"

"I think so. Which is your favourite?"

"I like them all. They're all good-looking," grinned Eric.

They were both wearing their sunglasses as the sun was beating down. It was a lovely day. Wild slid the disc in.

"Let's have a sing-along," suggested Wild. "It's good to have a sing-along. But you must know it's going to be very dangerous where we are going. So stay close behind me at all times."

"Ok," agreed the spy puppy, "but I can look after myself."

They drove for miles until they saw a 'SERVICES' sign. There were a lot of parking places and the station looked quiet, too quiet for Wild's liking. Eric got out and offered to get the drinks. Wild told him to get a bottle of dog water and not to forget the toilet sign. Eric set off and Wild, feeling a little tired, got into the back of the car and fell asleep.

In the shop, curiously, there was nobody around. Eric picked up two bottles of dog water and left two bones on the till. Uneasy he set off quickly back to the car. As he reached it he threw his arms in the air with a bottle in each hand crying, "Yo-ho, Wild, I've got a drink for you." As he said it a helicopter flew above Wild's car. It was Shifty and Bandy!

Eric looked around to see there must have been at least fifty black cars. He jumped into the driver's seat, started the car and pressed the turbo switch. He shot onto the motorway, but he had all the black cars behind him. He also had seven helicopters above.

Eric thought to himself that the tailor had been right.

This was going to be the best car chase ever. He put his sunglasses on and the chase was on. Wild was fast asleep in the back. Eric had to do it all himself. The helicopters dived at him and the cars kept nudging his bumper.

The heat was on, but this was not a problem for Eric. He was one of the best drivers around.

The chase went on for miles and Eric was struggling to lose them. Suddenly Wild's car started to splutter. It was running out of fuel. Eric tapped the fuel gauge, as he had seen this in films, but it didn't help. They were going to have to hope that by some miracle, they could outrun the black cars before the car conked out.

Eric hit the motorway. There were fifty Jaguars and seven helicopters behind them. He saw signs for Monte Carlo and thought he had better come up with a plan. The cars were getting closer and closer. He saw a 'SERVICES' sign and thought this was his way out. The cars were nudging his bumper and the helicopters were diving at him.

He decided it was time to make his getaway so he got into the middle of the road and pressed the turbo switch. Zoom! Eric was off at a high speed leaving everybody behind. He was going so fast he nearly missed the turn for the services but managed to get in and park.

He looked down to the back seat where Wild was still asleep and shouted, "A bottle of dog water, Wild?"

"Yes, please," said Wild waking up, "What's going on?"

"Not a lot," replied Eric. "All the cars and helicopters went past us on the motorway."

Wild sat up. "I must have dozed off. Come on we have a long journey ahead of us. By the way, what are you doing in the driver's seat?"

"Oh, I just wanted to see what it was like."

Wild climbed into the driver's seat and Eric got into the puppy seat.

"Ok, let's go; it's going to be a long day," said Wild. They pulled back onto the motorway.

It was very sunny. Wild turned the radio on and they began to sing songs in French and laughed at each other. They hadn't driven far when they saw a sign 'Monte Carlo 10 km'.

"But we've just set off," said Wild, scratching his head.

Eric smiled. "Pull up here and just look at that view of Monte Carlo. It is beautiful."

As he spoke Wild's phone that works on the moon, rang. Wild answered it.

"Hello," said the Chief of Dogs in French.

"What happened to you at the Eiffel Tower?" asked Wild.

"Well, er, I had to see a dog about a man," replied the Chief.

"You ran you mean?" asked Wild.

The Chief told them they were booked in at the Carlton hotel and were going to the Casino in Casino Square. He told them to meet Calor Gas there and hand over the two million bones to release Hat Dog.

"Well, it's not going to be that simple," said Wild.

"Yes it is," said the Chief. "Just give Calor Gas the bones and you will see Hat Dog."

"Ok, I'll speak soon. Good bye," said Wild.

"Plastic duck!" he shouted when he'd put the phone down.

"Who was that?" asked Eric.

"The Chief of Dogs – speaking French.

"Let's just have a few more minutes looking at this view of Monte Carlo," said Wild. "Oh and we are booked into the Carlton."

"What's it like?"

"It's beautiful with sea views. Nothing but the best for spy dogs."

They jumped back into the car and drove down the mountain road towards Monte Carlo with their sunglasses on and the music turned up loudly.

"This is one of the best places I have ever been," said Eric. "It's beautiful. Just look at the boats and cars. There must be some of the richest dogs in the world here."

"Yes," said Wild. "It's the playground of the rich. Let's check into the hotel. We have a few hours before we meet Calor Gas. Let's go out on a power boat. I have an idea."

They drove along the main road towards the Carlton. It

was next to the beach where the dogs played and sunbathed. They pulled up outside the hotel and were greeted by the manager.

"Welcome to the Carlton, Monte Carlo," he said. "It's a real pleasure to meet you, Mr. Wild."

Wild threw his keys to the manager asking him to park his car. He explained they would be back in an hour as they had a little job to do.

Wild and Eric strolled towards the harbour.

"What are we doing?" asked Eric.

"We are going to have some fun with Shifty and Bandy" said Wild. As they reached the boats Twig appeared from behind one.

"What are you doing here?" asked Wild. "and how did you get here before us?"

"I took the train," replied Twig.

"I see. Have you got me a boat?" demanded Wild.

"It's a bit like a power boat, but smaller and Wild," added Twig, "D insists you give Calor Gas the bones if you still have them."

"Yes, of course," agreed wild. "So where is this boat?"

"Follow me," said Twig, leading them to the water's edge. "There she is. She's a beauty."

"It's a dinghy and hardly a beauty," argued Wild.

"Yes," said Twig, "but it's remote controlled and you can send it out with Shifty and Bandy following. Then you can get on with rescuing Hat Dog."

"What a good idea," said Wild. "We will put cardboard cut-outs of us on board before we send it out."

"Here they are," said Twig. "I've already had them made."

"That was handy," said Wild. Come on, let's send it off now."

The dinghy set off at full speed out of the harbour. At the same moment they saw a power boat set off with Shifty and Bandy in hot pursuit.

"They've taken the bait," said Wild, "and look, they haven't had a wash yet. I think that will change, don't you?"

"Right. Pay attention, Wild," ordered Twig. "This is to go right and this is to go left."

"Yes, I understand that, Twig. Now give me the control."

Wild started to drive the boat. He sent it from one side of the harbour to the other with the cardboard cut-outs which had big smiles on their faces. Shifty and Bandy followed the dinghy; Wild was really playing with them and decided to keep them out there for a long time.

He noticed two little puppies playing nearby and had an idea. He went over to them and asked if they would like to play a little game.

"Yes," said one, "it's Mike Wild, isn't it?"

"It is," said Wild, passing over the remote control. "I want you to steer that boat in a figure of eight with Shifty and Bandy right behind it."

"Yes," replied the puppies. "And thanks, Wild. You are the best."

Twig looked at Wild, "That's my boat you're giving away."

The puppies were laughing and joking while they were steering the dinghy with the remote control.

"Yes, I know," said Wild then turned to Eric, "That will keep Shifty and Bandy busy for a while. Come on; let's go to the hotel." They set off.

"I hope all the gadgets I have given you are still in one piece," shouted Twig

"Yes, of course," replied Wild.

# CHAPTER FOURTEEN

*Calor Gas' mountain top villa, Monte Carlo.*

Meanwhile at his mountain top villa Calor Gas was talking to Hat Dog.

"In a few hours we will have two million bones and will live happily ever after."

"That's wonderful," she said, "because I do love you, Calor Gas."

"Do you?" he asked. "I love you and I will be a better dog than Mike Wild. We will get married when we have the bones."

"Yes, of course," she agreed.

He walked out onto his balcony which overlooked Monte

Carlo and shouted, "The Dog who loves me!"

# CHAPTER FIFTEEN

*The Carlton Hotel, Monte Carlo.*

Wild and Eric were just entering the hotel.

"What was that?" asked Eric. "Was it someone shouting?"

"It sounded like 'the dog who loves me,'" replied Wild, "but they are all a bit mad here."

"Come on, Eric," said Wild, "let's check into our room and get the bones and our suits from the car. We have a big night ahead of us."

They walked over to the car and got the briefcase with the bones in and their clothes then went back into the hotel reception where they were greeted again by the manager.

"Mr. Wild, back so soon. And who is your friend?"

"This is Eric, a spy puppy," said Wild. "Can I order a

biscuit for him because he is only a very young puppy?"

"Of course," agreed the manager. "Will there be anything else?"

"Please would you post this," he handed over the tracking device, "to London." He turned to Eric, "Twig will love that!"

"What's the address?" asked the manager.

"Twig at Control Centre, London," replied Wild.

"Your chief has booked you in, but not into the room you usually have," explained the manager. "It is one of our cheaper rooms. Should I put you in our penthouse overlooking the sea and Monte Carlo? It's our best."

"Yes, of course," said Wild. "I am the best spy dog in the world and I only have the best. And please send me up a bottle of the best dog water you have. Come on, Eric; let's go up to the room."

"I don't need a dog biscuit," said Eric, "and I can't sleep on a bed like you."

"Yes, you can," Wild replied and walked over to the lift,

jumped in and pressed the button for the penthouse.

The door opened at the top floor and they went over to their

room which opened automatically. As they walked in Wild's

phone that works on the moon, rang.

"Hello," said Wild.

"Hello, this is the Chief of Dogs in France. Listen, I will say this only once. I have entered you in a poker game at the Casino. It's one million bones to enter and you will be playing Calor Gas. You must lose to him both times and give him the bones so we can get Hat Dog back. Do I make myself clear? You must lose to Calor Gas. Ok, I will see you and Eric at the Casino at 8.00pm. We have a table booked for dinner, so don't be late."

"Plastic duck," said Wild and put the phone down.

"Who was that?" asked Eric. "And why did you say 'plastic duck'?"

"Because he is French," explained Wild. "It was the Chief of Dogs and we are meeting him tonight at the Casino, so let's have a shower and put our suits on."

Half an hour later they were both wearing tuxedoes and looked the smartest dogs in town. Eric had his espadrilles on and asked Wild, "Can you go into the Casino with trainers on?"

"Of course we can," replied Wild.

They walked onto their balcony and looked at the sea views, then at each other and shouted, "Come on; let's get Hat Dog back!" and clicked their paws together. They could see that Shifty and Bandy were still chasing the remote controlled boat. They both laughed.

It was time to meet the Chief and they walked through Monte Carlo admiring the boats and cars. A rich dog who lived nearby asked Wild if he was Mike Wild.

"I certainly am," replied Wild.

Eric put his paws to his face and laughed

They finally reached Casino Square. It was a beautiful place Eric's face lit up. He had never seen a place like it.

"Come on," said Wild, "we have a job to do."

They reached the entrance.

“No trainers, sir,” shouted a doordog.

“Are you having a laugh? My name is Mike Wild.”

“Look,” came the reply, “if your name’s not John you are not coming in.”

“My name’s John,” said Eric and the doordog let him in. “See you later, Wild,” said the spy puppy.

Wild said, “Look, I’ve come a long way.”

“Listen, dog breath,” said the doordog, “if your name’s not John, you don’t get in!”

Wild stood back wondering what to do. Eric opened a window and shouted, “Tell him your name’s John.”

Just then another dog came to the door and said his name was John. “If your name’s not Mike, you are not coming in,” announced the doordog.

Wild heard this and said, “My name’s Mike.”

“Come in then,” said the doordog.

Mike walked through the door thinking, “What a stupid

dog!"

The Chief and Eric were waiting at the bar; Mike walked over to them.

"What's with the dog on the door then?"

"He thinks he is Arnold Schwarzenegger," said the Chief.

"Who?"

"Oh, it doesn't matter," said the Chief. "Now pay attention, Wild, would you like a drink?"

"Yes, please," said Wild, "a glass of dog water with ice."

The Chief ordered three and the bardog told them their table was ready.

The three of them sat down and the bar dog asked for their food order. Wild said that he would have a three egg omelette and wanted the chef to know it was for him. Eric ordered crumpet and beans and the Chief wanted French onions.

"French onions? You must be mad!" said Wild.

"Now pay attention, Wild," said the Chief. "When we have

eaten we are going to the poker table and your orders are to lose both paws and two million bones to Calor Gas so he will release Hat Dog." He continued, "No funny business, Wild. Your job is to take her back to London where D is waiting. You are to fly to London, so I will have your car keys, if you don't mind."

"Why do you want my car keys?"

"It's not me," said the Chief, "I am under strict orders to take your keys now."

Wild handed over the keys saying, "Don't press any switches on that car."

The Chief thanked him and left the keys on the table. Wild and Eric looked at each other and smiled. The food arrived and everybody began to tuck in. As they ate Eric slipped the keys into his pocket without the Chief spotting him. Wild saw him and smiled.

It didn't take long to finish the meal and Wild said it was the best omelette he had ever tasted. "Ok, Chief, I think you should get the bill," said Wild. He and Eric jumped up and left the Chief eating his onions. They walked over to the Casino entrance. The Casino manager greeted them. "Mr. Wild, I believe."

"Yes."

"Calor Gas is waiting for you, sir? Have you got the bones to play with?"

Wild handed them over and asked to be taken to Calor Gas.

"Of course, Mr. Wild."

Wild turned to Eric and told him to watch out for Shifty, Bandy and Calor Gas too.

The manager opened the two big doors and they followed him in. There was Calor Gas – with Hat Dog. Wild looked into her eyes and smiled. She smiled back.

"What's going on?" demanded Calor Gas, leaping up from his chair.

"Come on, fatty," said Wild, "let's play."

"Who are you calling 'fatty', dog breath?" retorted Calor Gas.

"Dog breath?" said Wild.

"Now then, you two," said Hat Dog, "You are here to play poker, not have a shouting match."`

"Ok, you are right," said Wild. "Let's play." They both sat down.

"Ok, dogs," said the manager, "the game tonight is set at one million bones the paw." As he spoke Shifty and Bandy ran into the room. Because they had run out of fuel they had had to swim ashore. They were washed now, but covered in seaweed. They looked at Wild and growled. Wild and Eric just laughed. "Is everyone here?" asked the manager.

"Yes," said the Chief as he entered closing the doors behind him.

"Well, let's play." The first two cards went to Wild. He looked at them.

"Stick."

They all looked at Wild as the next two cards went to Calor Gas. He also stuck. The two dogs looked at each other.

"Turn your cards over, please, sir," the manager asked

Calor Gas.

Then he asked Wild to do the same. To his surprise Wild had won. This was not supposed to happen and everyone looked at Wild. Hat Dog said she was going to get some more drinks and stood up. As she rose she picked up Wild's briefcase with the bones. Then she left the room. The Chief kicked Wild's chair and whispered in his ear.

"You have got to lose. Give Calor Gas the bones or you will never see Hat Dog again."

Calor Gas, Shifty and Bandy all looked at Wild and growled. "Let's play again," said the manager and gave Wild two cards. Wild looked at them, then at everyone around. "Stick." Calor Gas was given his cards and asked to turn them over. He had a good paw. But what did Wild have? All eyes were on Wild as he turned over his cards. Much to his surprise he had won again. The Chief fell over!

The manager asked Calor Gas for two million bones. Wild took out his smoke pen and pressed the button. Smoke filled the room. Wild dropped to his paws and crawled over to get Calor Gas. Shifty and Bandy were coughing and swinging their arms wildly shouting, "Where are you, Wild?" Wild grabbed Calor Gas who quickly shook him off then ran to the fire escape and started up the stairs with Wild right behind him. Step after step wild was on his tail. They reached the roof.

Meanwhile downstairs the smoke had cleared and Shifty and Bandy were chasing Eric down the stairs.

Upstairs Calor Gas opened the door onto the roof. Wild was still with him. Calor Gas ran towards his helicopter which took off with Calor Gas jumping onto the rails and hanging on by his paws.

"I will get you next time," he shouted at Wild. "I will be back."

Wild stood on the roof with his tongue hanging out of the side of his mouth.

"Next time," he said to himself. "But now I must get back to Eric."

Downstairs, step by step, Shifty and Bandy were getting closer to Eric. He reached the bottom of the stairs and burst through the exit door. There was a 1964 Aston Martin DB5 with the best looking puppy driving. She kicked the passenger door open and told him to get in. It was Eric's lucky day. He jumped in and they set off at high speed. Shifty and Bandy watched him drive away.

"We will get you," they shouted. Then they thought of the tracking device. They could follow using that and Calor Gas would be proud of them.

Wild walked down the stairs of the Casino and saw the Chief lying on a stretcher.

"What have you done, Wild?" he asked. "You have no Hat Dog, no two million bones and you have destroyed this room. D will have our tails over this."

Wild looked around and saw a plastic duck on a table. He told the Chief to open his mouth wide and popped the duck in. Then he turned to the ambulance driver saying, "He is mad, you know. Take him to the mental hospital.

"Mr. Wild," said the Casino manager, "Calor is barred from here - and he owes you two million bones. "It's only bones," replied Wild.

When he got up next morning he went for a walk along

the beach. He strolled along, with his trainers on his paws, wondering what had happened to Hat Dog and the two million bones. His phone rang – the one that works on the moon with 'Hopelessly Devoted to You' as a ring tone.

"Hello," he answered.

"Now pay attention Wild, it's Twig. I've just had a nice surprise in the post – a tracking device. Ten minutes later two bad dogs called Shifty Eyes and Bandy Legs arrived. They are now safely behind bars. So thank you, Wild, and don't forget to bring my car back in one piece. One other thing. The Chief of Dogs in France has been checked into the mental hospital. I don't suppose you know anything about that?"

"No," said Wild, "and good bye."

As he finished the call he heard someone shouting. It was the hotel manager telling him that his car had been found at the airport with the keys in. He added that there was a message from Eric to let him know he was fine and back in Paris with a new puppy friend and he thanked Wild.

Wild continued his walk along the beach and stopped to pick up a sea shell. He put it to his ear and could hear music. It was Café de Mar. Then he knew were Hat Dog was. She was at the Café de Mar in Ibiza.

# CHAPTER SIXTEEN

*Café De Mar, Ibiza, Spain*

He was on the next flight to Ibiza. He took a taxi to the bar. As he walked in he could see the briefcase with a bottle of dog water and two glasses. He poured himself a drink then heard a voice.

"Wild."

"Hat Dog," he said looking round, "did you plan this?"

"No," she said, "and please pour me a drink."

His phone that works on the moon, rang. Hat Dog smiled.

"Hello," said D. "Where are the Queen's bones and where is Hat Dog?"

"Sir, you are breaking up, sir, sir, sir…" said Wild and put the phone down.

"Now, Hat Dog, where were we?" he asked. "Oh, yes."

He gave her a drink.

"Here is the best sunset view in the world."

Then he kissed her lips.

## Synopsis

In a few years from now, man no longer exists and the world is ruled by dogs. They have human like tendencies and live in the world as we know it. They wear the same clothes and stand on their back two legs. Their currency is bones.

The story is about a dog called Hat Dog, a famous model who is kidnapped by Calor Gas, an evil dog. He holds her for ransom. There is one dog who can save her. His name is Mike Wild, the best spy dog in the world, or so he says. Wild has to exchange one million bones for her release in Monte Carlo, but there are many twists and turns on the way, such as stopping in Paris and using his gadgets. With a little help from his friends he gets the job done!

Printed in Great
Britain
by Amazon

32216188R00059